LONDON

Richard Platt

Illustrated by Manuela Cappon

KINGFISHER

London

In modern, noisy London, English words are everywhere, but each voice sounds different. Visitors are baffled by native London words, but there's no mistaking the American twang of businessmen in a smart restaurant. Their waitress speaks perfect English, but with an accent from elsewhere in Europe, and an Asian accent echoes from the kitchen. For London is not just the capital of Britain. It is the centre of the English-speaking world and a flourishing European city.

Scotland

Glasgow   EDINBURGH

North Sea

Northern Ireland

BELFAST

UNITED KINGDOM

Atlantic Ocean

Irish Sea

REPUBLIC OF IRELAND

DUBLIN   Liverpool   Leeds

Manchester

England

Wales   Birmingham

CARDIFF   Bristol

LONDON

English Channel

FRANCE

North America

Europe

Asia

Africa

South America

Australia

Throughout its long history, London has always been a place where people have met, mixed and mingled. Spreading across a winding river on an island in the corner of Europe, the city first prospered almost 2,000 years ago. Success attracted jealous or greedy rivals, and invaders intent on either conquering or destroying the city.

Over the centuries, Britain won empires in America, Africa and Asia. London thrived with each conquest. As each empire crumbled, London in turn declined – but never too far. In the 20th century, the city survived economic disaster, war-time bombs and terrorist attacks. Today, it is looking towards a brighter future once again.

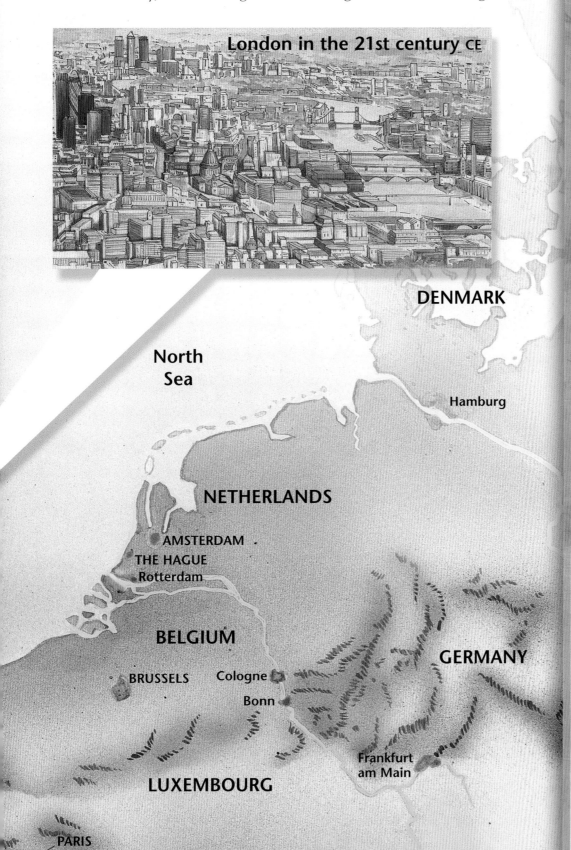

London in the 21st century CE

DENMARK

North Sea

Hamburg

NETHERLANDS

AMSTERDAM
THE HAGUE
Rotterdam

BELGIUM

BRUSSELS   Cologne
         Bonn

GERMANY

Frankfurt
am Main

LUXEMBOURG

PARIS

London timeline

300000BCE Ice grips Britain: glaciers block the River Thames, forcing it southwards to where it flows today

50000BCE Hunters chase woolly mammoths and rhinoceroses along the banks of the Thames

3500BCE Using stone axes, families fell trees on the banks of the Thames; they build a village

1100BCE The riverbank dwellers honour water gods by casting their finest bronze tools into the Thames

800BCE Celtic people from central Europe settle beside the Thames

43CE An invading Roman army bridges the Thames, and lays the first stones of a new town, Londinium

60CE Led by the warrior-queen Boudicca, Celts destroy Londinium

225CE Romans surround their rebuilt city with a defensive wall

407CE Romans abandon Londinium

500CE Saxon people from Germany have started a new town, Lundenwic, to the west of the old walled city

851CE Danish Vikings attack Lundenwic; more raids follow

1078CE Norman duke William 'the Conqueror' orders a tower (castle) built in London after capturing the city, and all of England, 12 years previously

1209CE A stone bridge across the Thames replaces earlier wooden ones

1348CE One-third of Londoners die as the Black Death infects the city

1476CE William Caxton begins to print books at Westminster

1599CE William Shakespeare's company of actors builds the Globe theatre on the Thames' south bank

1649CE King Charles I is executed as civil war tears England apart

1660CE Londoner Samuel Pepys starts a diary that will make him famous

1666CE Fire destroys nearly all of the buildings within London's walls

1675CE Work begins on the rebuilding of St Paul's cathedral

1809CE First gas lamps light the streets

1825CE London becomes the largest city in the world

1851CE London hosts the Great Exhibition in Hyde Park

1863CE First underground trains run

1940CE World War II bombings destroy London buildings but kill few

2005CE London is selected to host the Olympic Games in the summer of 2012

What do these dates mean?

'CE' means Common Era. This is the period of measured time that begins with 1CE (or AD1).

'BCE' means Before Common Era, and refers to any dates before 1CE. For example, 100BCE means '100 years before the Common Era'.

300000 BCE
50000 BCE
1000 BCE
1CE
100CE
500CE
1000CE
1500CE
2000CE

Contents

The pages that follow trace London's long, dramatic history. Reading them, you will see how it was once just a riverside camp, and later a thriving town. You will discover how it was conquered and burned to the ground. And you will witness London flourishing once again, growing into a large, prosperous, multicultural city.

3500BCE   **60CE**   **851CE**   **1216CE**

43CE   **225CE**   **1091CE**

London in 43CE

River Fleet   Walbrook stream

N

Today's London
London 43CE
River Thames

A locator map shows how the city is growing over time, and where each scene takes place.

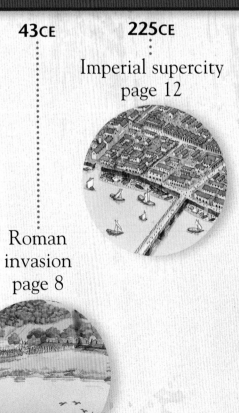

The age of print
page 22

Georgian London
page 30

Fame and
fashion
page 38

The Great Fire
page 26

Industrial giant
page 34

1476CE   **1666**CE   **1783**CE   **1900**CE   **1963**CE

1348CE   **1602**CE   **1707**CE   **1851**CE   **1940**CE   *Today*

Shakespeare's London
page 24

The Blitz
page 36

Plague!
page 20

From the
ashes
page 28

The Great
Exhibition
page 32

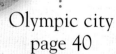

Olympic city
page 40

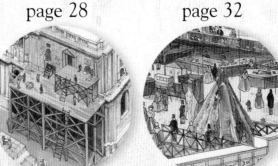

Neolithic camp 3500BCE

wolves prowl in the dense undergrowth

On a low, muddy bank in the middle of the shallow, winding Thames river, stealthy hunters hurl stone-tipped spears at a group of plump geese. But the geese fly off, honking with alarm. The hunters have missed this time, but they will not go hungry. There are plenty more birds – as well as fish, and bigger game such as deer – near to their village of simple wooden huts.

Hunters have been wandering along the Thames riverbanks for as many as 200,000 years, but these Neolithic (New Stone Age) people are among the first to stop and clear the woodland. As well as hunting and collecting plant foods, as their ancestors did, they have also begun to grow crops and herd animals in the spaces they have cleared.

The Neolithic people are creating and decorating clay pots, and shaping flint chips into razor-sharp tools.

the shallow Thames river winds slowly through reedy islands and sandbanks

They have built their village on a high gravel bank. It has good soil and is better drained than the surrounding marsh. It stays dry even when the river floods. The water here is shallow and easy to cross. In the future these benefits will attract more and more families to the spot. Some will settle here for good, marking the beginning of the place we now call 'London'.

London in 3500BCE

River Fleet

Walbrook stream

N

Today's London
London 3500BCE
River Thames

possible Neolithic site

wild deer

boar forage for food

woodland covers all of the higher land

burning trees and bushes clears land for settlement

Houses built from poles and mud, and roofed with straw thatch, are simple but warm and dry.

the roofs are thatched with reeds or leaves

the huts have wooden frames

this stream is now known as Walbrook stream

a muddy mixture (daub) covers walls woven with sticks (wattles)

sheep are raised for milk and wool, but not meat

the high riverbank keeps the settlement above free from floods

wild ducks

everyone knows how to make useful tools from stone

fish from the river will be grilled over hot embers from the fire

some Neolithic people still lead the same nomadic (wandering) lives as did their ancestors

hunters have tamed dogs to help them catch animals for food

animal skins provide clothes for everyone

woven wooden walkways cross marshland and shallow water

The riverbank people are religious. They have marked their sacred path with a cursus – a pair of ditches.

7

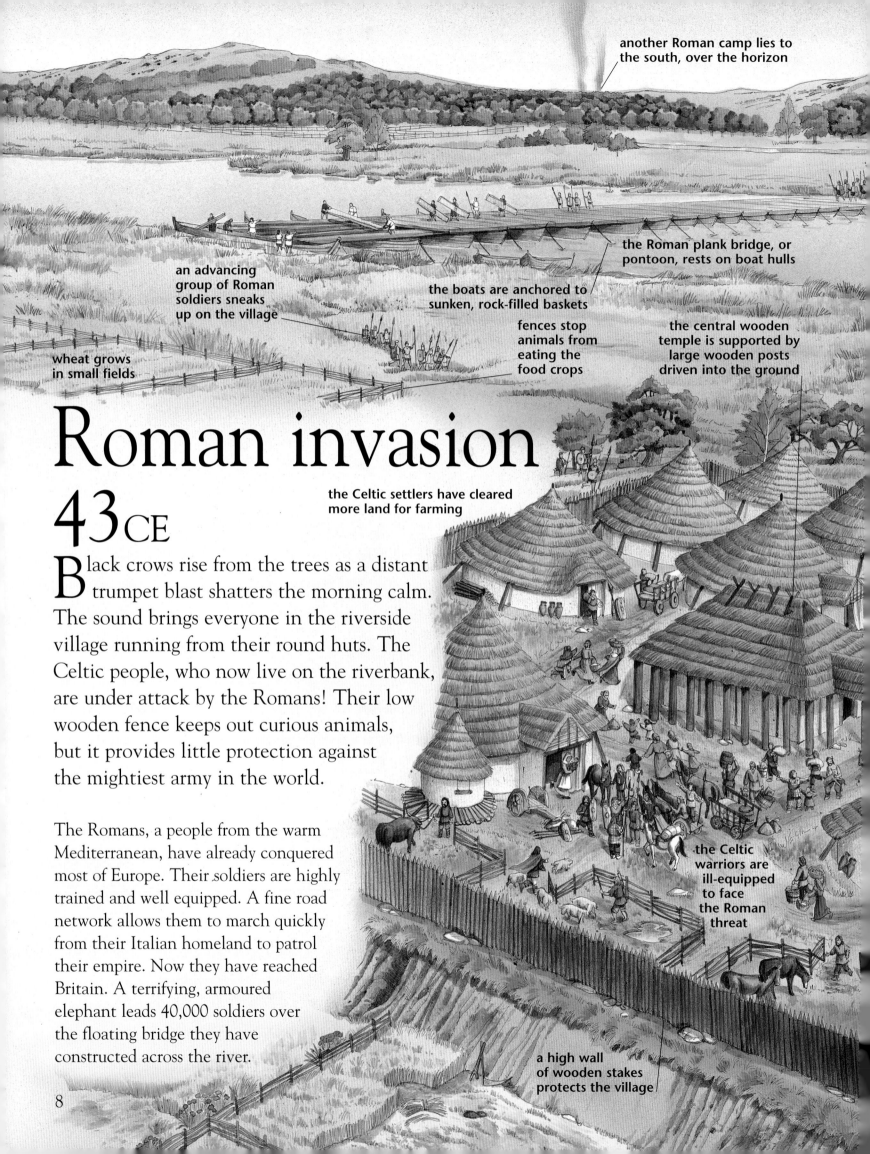

another Roman camp lies to the south, over the horizon

the Roman plank bridge, or pontoon, rests on boat hulls

an advancing group of Roman soldiers sneaks up on the village

the boats are anchored to sunken, rock-filled baskets

fences stop animals from eating the food crops

the central wooden temple is supported by large wooden posts driven into the ground

wheat grows in small fields

Roman invasion
43 CE

Black crows rise from the trees as a distant trumpet blast shatters the morning calm. The sound brings everyone in the riverside village running from their round huts. The Celtic people, who now live on the riverbank, are under attack by the Romans! Their low wooden fence keeps out curious animals, but it provides little protection against the mightiest army in the world.

The Romans, a people from the warm Mediterranean, have already conquered most of Europe. Their soldiers are highly trained and well equipped. A fine road network allows them to march quickly from their Italian homeland to patrol their empire. Now they have reached Britain. A terrifying, armoured elephant leads 40,000 soldiers over the floating bridge they have constructed across the river.

the Celtic settlers have cleared more land for farming

the Celtic warriors are ill-equipped to face the Roman threat

a high wall of wooden stakes protects the village

a temporary
Roman camp

the Roman soldiers have
pitched their leather tents

the war elephant is
a Roman weapon
of terror

soldiers wait to
cross the river

The villagers know how to defend themselves. They have iron swords and helmets. Other Celtic tribes to the southeast of this settlement held back the Roman army for two whole days. The women grab their children, and their most valuable possessions, and flee. The warriors who remain soon realize they cannot win. They surrender without a fight. Over the next few years the Romans will conquer all of England and Wales.

villagers flee
with whatever
they can carry

The Romans bring elephants to war, to frighten enemies who may not have seen the animals before.

pottery and fine
metal vessels are
precious possessions

In ceremonies to honour water gods, priests toss valuable metal objects into the Thames.

animals now graze
on vegetation in the
cursus ditches

pigs
feast on
fallen acorns

London in 43CE

River Fleet
Walbrook stream

N

Today's London
London 43CE
River Thames

possible Celtic site

9

Boudicca attacks!

60CE

Under Roman control, solid houses replace the Celtic huts on the riverbank. By 60CE the small town is a centre for trading on land and water. A stone forum (market building) stands on a main road. Ships from France and Italy sail up the Thames to unload wine at the quayside next to a sturdy bridge. The Romans of 'Londinium' feel safe. They have not even built a wall to defend their town.

They pay a high price for their over-confidence. The Iceni, a tribe of Celtic people from eastern England, have rebelled. Romans have whipped their queen, Boudicca, and abused her daughters. Now the Iceni people want vengeance. Their warriors advance to Londinium. Terrified of what is to come, the city's governor, Suetonius, orders his people to flee.

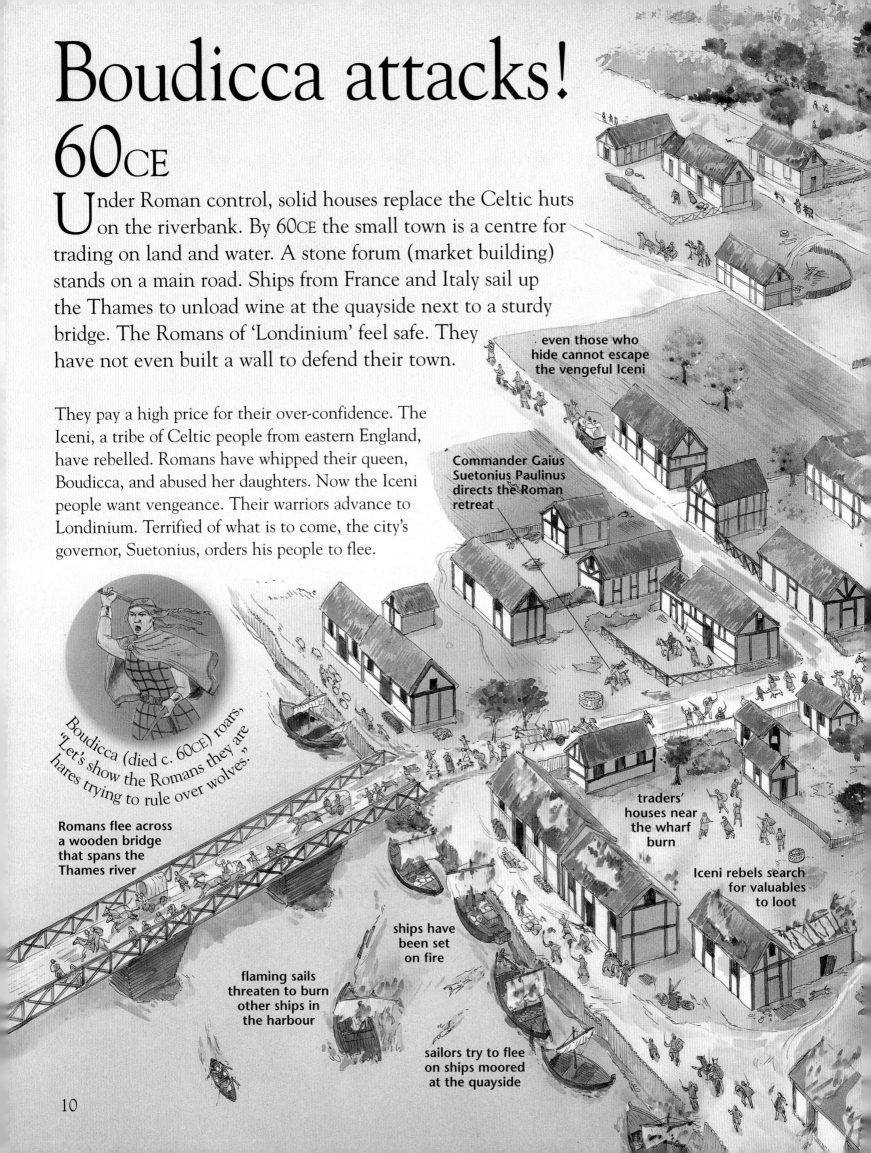

Boudicca (died c. 60CE) roars, "Let's show the Romans they are hares trying to rule over wolves."

even those who hide cannot escape the vengeful Iceni

Commander Gaius Suetonius Paulinus directs the Roman retreat

traders' houses near the wharf burn

Iceni rebels search for valuables to loot

Romans flee across a wooden bridge that spans the Thames river

ships have been set on fire

flaming sails threaten to burn other ships in the harbour

sailors try to flee on ships moored at the quayside

10

London in 60CE

River Fleet
Walbrook stream
N

Today's London
London 60CE
River Thames

there are no walls or ditches to defend the city from attack

Iceni warriors pick off the Roman stragglers as they attempt to flee Londinium on foot.

Iceni warriors push a burning haywagon down a hill, towards Roman buildings

a network of well-built roads makes escape easy and quick

most residents fled hours earlier, leaving streets empty

the forum (marketplace) is the only solid stone building in the settlement

Iceni warriors set fire to buildings

Queen Boudicca riding on her chariot

captured Romans face horrible deaths

wood-and-thatch houses burn fiercely

The streets are almost empty when the Celtic army attacks. They take their revenge ruthlessly. They torture and kill any Romans they find, and steal anything of value. Finally, they set the town on fire. However, Roman troops stationed in Londinium have escaped. They soon hit back at the rebellious Britons. Defeated, Boudicca poisons herself, and the Romans return to rebuild their shattered town.

11

Today's London
London 225CE
River Thames

River Fleet
Walbrook stream
N
Southwark

London's six gates defend the city's entrances. They have space for war catapults on their roofs.

a fortress houses Londinium's garrison (soldier-guards)

Cripplegate

Aldersgate

River Fleet

Newgate

Cheapside public baths

the amphitheatre also stages plays, and military troops train here

Ludgate

Temple of Mithras

a strong wall surrounds the city on the landward side

the Romans worship their many gods at several different temples

beneath the streets, buried pipes supply drinking water

Londinium's governor lives in a fine palace

Imperial supercity 225CE

A new city has grown and prospered on the ash and cinders of the town that Boudicca and her warriors destroyed. By the third century CE, Londinium is the great capital of Roman Britain. Half of all the country's roads fan out from here. The city has even spread to the south bank of the River Thames, where houses and shops cluster around the end of the timber bridge.

ships bring luxury goods from distant parts of the Roman empire

a solid bridge provides a trade route to the south

Spring water supplies the public baths, and roaring furnaces keep the floors and pools nice and hot.

the bridge has allowed Londinium to spread to the south bank of the river

12

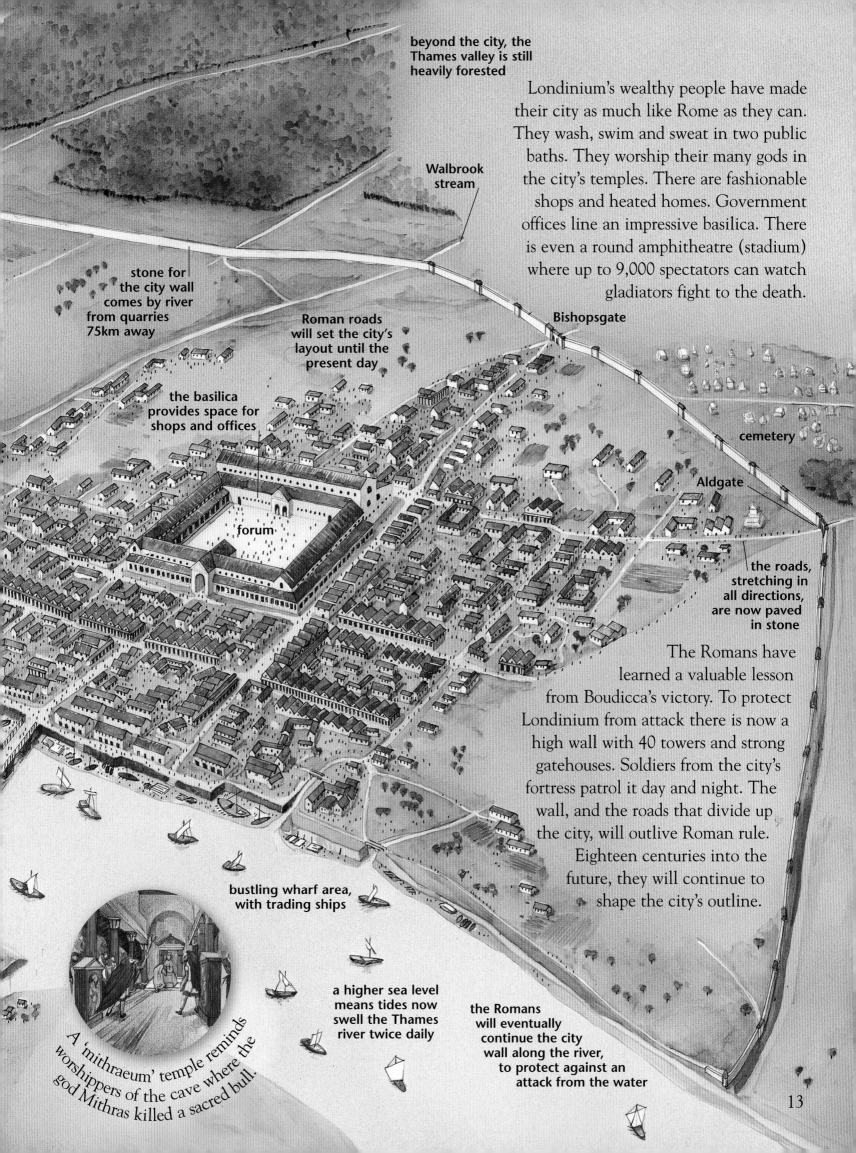

beyond the city, the Thames valley is still heavily forested

Walbrook stream

Londinium's wealthy people have made their city as much like Rome as they can. They wash, swim and sweat in two public baths. They worship their many gods in the city's temples. There are fashionable shops and heated homes. Government offices line an impressive basilica. There is even a round amphitheatre (stadium) where up to 9,000 spectators can watch gladiators fight to the death.

stone for the city wall comes by river from quarries 75km away

Roman roads will set the city's layout until the present day

Bishopsgate

the basilica provides space for shops and offices

cemetery

forum

Aldgate

the roads, stretching in all directions, are now paved in stone

The Romans have learned a valuable lesson from Boudicca's victory. To protect Londinium from attack there is now a high wall with 40 towers and strong gatehouses. Soldiers from the city's fortress patrol it day and night. The wall, and the roads that divide up the city, will outlive Roman rule. Eighteen centuries into the future, they will continue to shape the city's outline.

bustling wharf area, with trading ships

A 'mithraeum' temple reminds worshippers of the cave where the god Mithras killed a sacred bull.

a higher sea level means tides now swell the Thames river twice daily

the Romans will eventually continue the city wall along the river, to protect against an attack from the water

13

A Viking raid 851 CE

The rising tide washes them up the Thames – a huge fleet of ships with tall, terrifying warriors at the oars. The Vikings run ashore and attack like hungry wolves. These men are Danish pirates. Their repeated raids threaten the very survival of this small, riverside town and its Saxon people.

the Roman city wall

the Saxon houses are low, simple shelters

valuable livestock are herded away to the safety of fields to the north

the Saxon settlement is on the site of modern London's famous Covent Garden market

the riverside marketplace is already a centre for international trade

the tall Viking warriors are terrifying figures

as they leave, the Vikings start fires that will burn Lundenwic to the ground

the Lundenwic 'docks' are little more than plank jetties

the Vikings carry off the fit, young and beautiful to sell as slaves

Four centuries earlier, the Saxons came from Germany, taking over the region as Roman power weakened. They settled west of Londinium, building a riverside hamlet, named Lundenwic, and farming the land around it. A Christian people, they have built churches near to the river. The Viking invaders head for these buildings first. They know they will find rich booty in these sacred places.

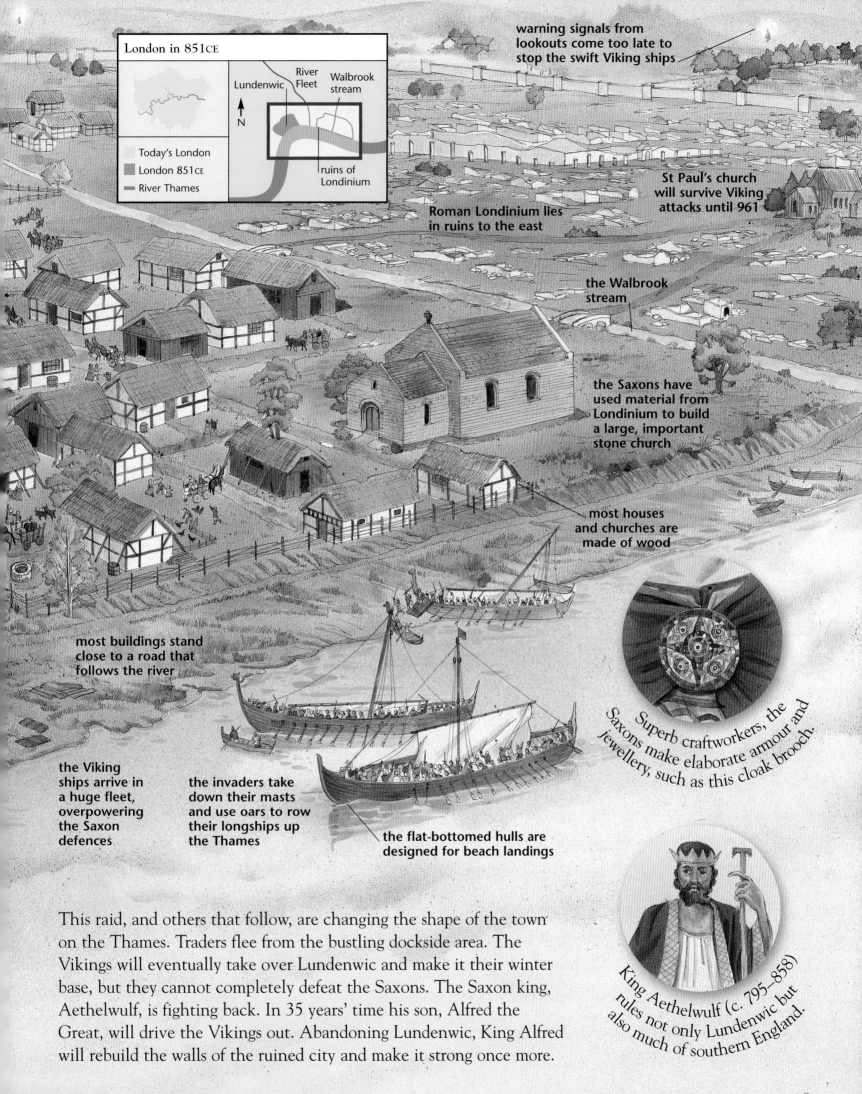

London in 851 CE

Today's London
London 851 CE
River Thames

Lundenwic · River Fleet · Walbrook stream

N

ruins of Londinium

warning signals from lookouts come too late to stop the swift Viking ships

Roman Londinium lies in ruins to the east

St Paul's church will survive Viking attacks until 961

the Walbrook stream

the Saxons have used material from Londinium to build a large, important stone church

most houses and churches are made of wood

most buildings stand close to a road that follows the river

Superb craftworkers, the Saxons make elaborate armour and jewellery, such as this cloak brooch.

the Viking ships arrive in a huge fleet, overpowering the Saxon defences

the invaders take down their masts and use oars to row their longships up the Thames

the flat-bottomed hulls are designed for beach landings

This raid, and others that follow, are changing the shape of the town on the Thames. Traders flee from the bustling dockside area. The Vikings will eventually take over Lundenwic and make it their winter base, but they cannot completely defeat the Saxons. The Saxon king, Aethelwulf, is fighting back. In 35 years' time his son, Alfred the Great, will drive the Vikings out. Abandoning Lundenwic, King Alfred will rebuild the walls of the ruined city and make it strong once more.

King Aethelwulf (c. 795–858) rules not only Lundenwic but also much of southern England.

15

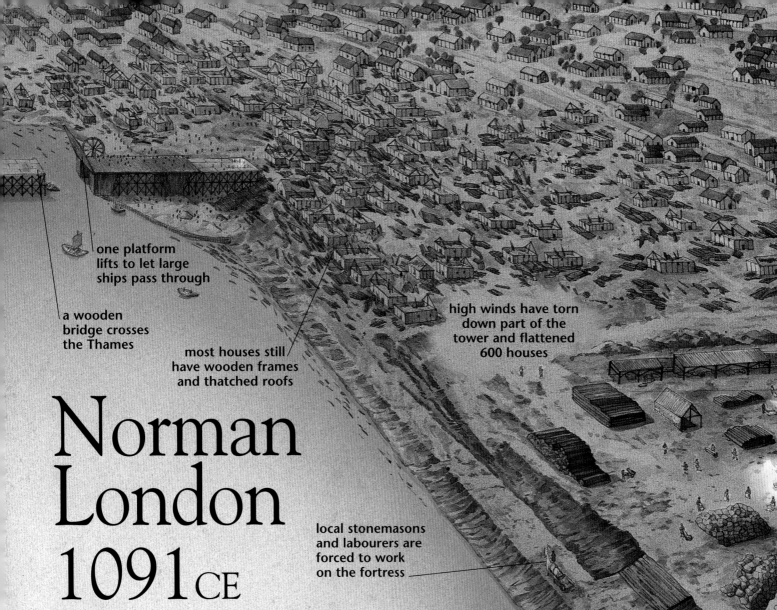

one platform lifts to let large ships pass through

a wooden bridge crosses the Thames

most houses still have wooden frames and thatched roofs

high winds have torn down part of the tower and flattened 600 houses

local stonemasons and labourers are forced to work on the fortress

the Normans transport stone from quarries in France

wooden posts have been used to turn muddy riverbanks into solid wharves

Norman London 1091 CE

On London's eastern corner, masons are toiling on a vast, tall castle. For once again London has new, foreign rulers. William of Normandy, France, invaded England a quarter of a century ago, in 1066. Renamed William 'the Conqueror', the French king strengthened his grip over England's fierce and restless people. The White Tower is simply the grandest among a chain of strongholds the Normans have constructed.

William made London England's capital, so he had to bring the city completely under his control. To the west, just outside the city walls, Westminster is now a centre for the law and the site of a royal palace. Inside the walls, merchants handle local and international trade. London is a religious centre, too, with many new churches and monasteries under construction.

A powerful gale rips through London in 1091, tearing off church roofs and damaging the bridge.

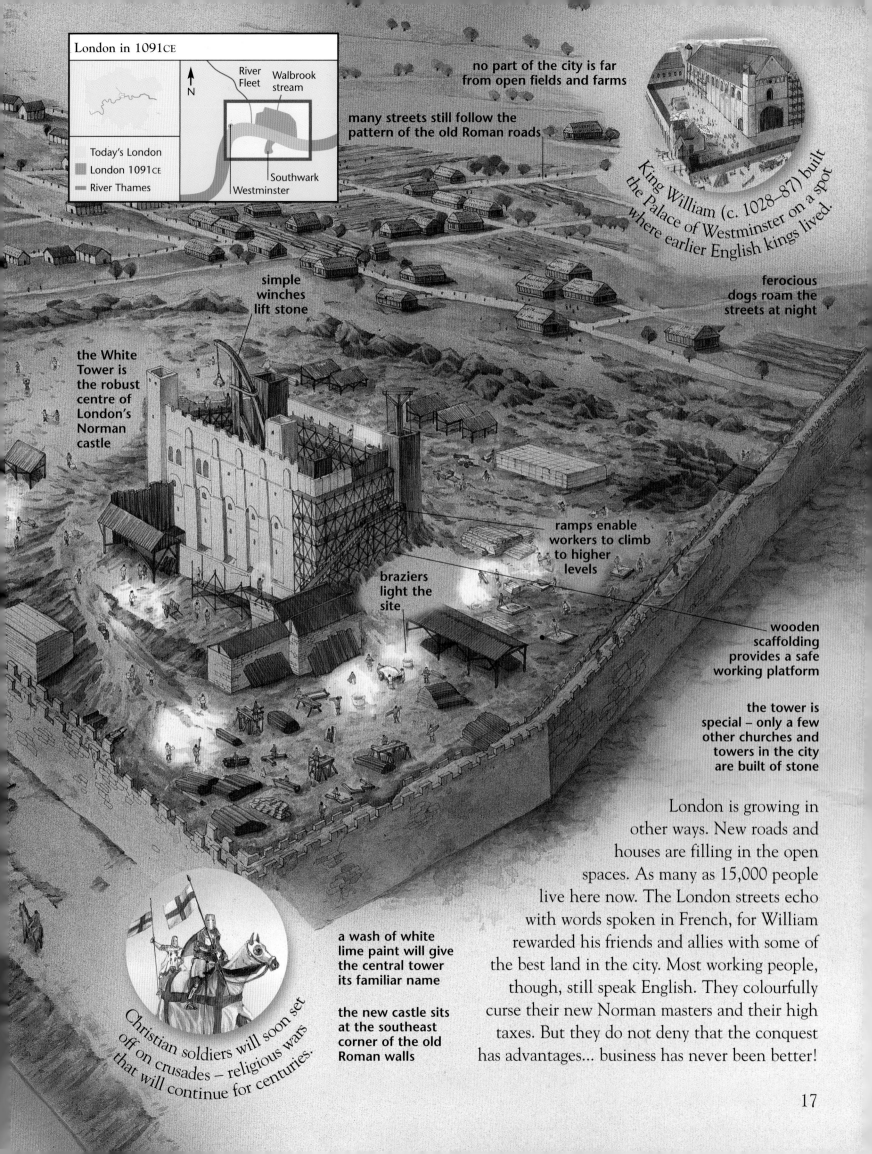

River Fleet
Walbrook stream

N

Today's London
London 1091CE
River Thames

Westminster
Southwark

no part of the city is far from open fields and farms

many streets still follow the pattern of the old Roman roads

King William (c. 1028–87) built the Palace of Westminster on a spot where earlier English kings lived.

ferocious dogs roam the streets at night

simple winches lift stone

the White Tower is the robust centre of London's Norman castle

ramps enable workers to climb to higher levels

braziers light the site

wooden scaffolding provides a safe working platform

the tower is special – only a few other churches and towers in the city are built of stone

London is growing in other ways. New roads and houses are filling in the open spaces. As many as 15,000 people live here now. The London streets echo with words spoken in French, for William rewarded his friends and allies with some of the best land in the city. Most working people, though, still speak English. They colourfully curse their new Norman masters and their high taxes. But they do not deny that the conquest has advantages... business has never been better!

Christian soldiers will soon set off on crusades – religious wars that will continue for centuries.

a wash of white lime paint will give the central tower its familiar name

the new castle sits at the southeast corner of the old Roman walls

Bridge of stone 1216CE

Since ancient times, Londoners have crossed the swirling, salty waters of the Thames river on wooden bridges. Wars, fires, floods, ice, gales and rot have destroyed them one after another. Then, in the 12th century, priest and bridge-master Peter de Colchurch decided it was time for something stronger and sturdier: a bridge made of stone.

London's new bridge was completed seven years ago, in 1209. Today, in the summer of 1216, it is at the centre of a political revolution. England's unpopular King John (1167–1216), is at war with his powerful barons. Weary of his hopeless leadership, they have invited the French king, Louis VIII (1187–1226), to take John's place as ruler. Louis and his knights pause briefly at the bridge gates, before crossing amid cheering crowds.

London's fine cathedral, St Paul's, will host the French king's welcome ceremony

colours from the bankside dye-works tint the water

London in 1216CE

Westminster | River Fleet | Walbrook stream

N

Today's London
London 1216CE
River Thames

St Paul's cathedral | Southwark

during Roman times, London began spreading out around the south end of the bridge

the neighbourhood on this side of the bridge is called Southwark, meaning 'southern fortress'

ferrymen take passengers across the Thames

most London houses are still built out of wood

house of the Bishop of Winchester

Southwark is built on what was once marshland

Soon after his arrival, Louis is declared king at a special ceremony inside St Paul's.

Southwark Priory

before the arrival of the French, the English king, John, fled across the bridge to Winchester

18

fireproof stone and tiled roofs are gradually replacing thatch

bridge-master Peter de Colchurch died before his work was complete, and his body was entombed inside St Thomas's chapel on the bridge

two Roman roads meet at the end of the bridge

a stone bridge has replaced the wooden river crossing

houses and shops cluster on either side of the narrow roadway

a noisy crowd begins to gather on the bridge

ships land fish, wine, grain and cloth at riverside wharves

London Bridge still has one span (platform) that opens to allow larger boats through

London's first mayor, Henry Fitz-Ailwyn, greets the French king at a stone gateway, at the south end of the bridge

Without the smell and sound of the water below them, the visitors would not know they are crossing a river. For houses and shops line the roadway, crowding in on them. Shopkeepers shout from doorways. Residents empty stinking chamber pots from their windows. Beggars plead for change and thieves eye the fat purses of the new arrivals. In fact, London Bridge gives the French king a vivid first glimpse of the noisy, smelly, violent, bustling city beyond.

Louis VIII has ridden 100km from the English coast

French knights carry the king's gold-and-blue royal emblem

One year ago, the barons forced King John to sign the Magna Carta and agree to the laws set out on it.

19

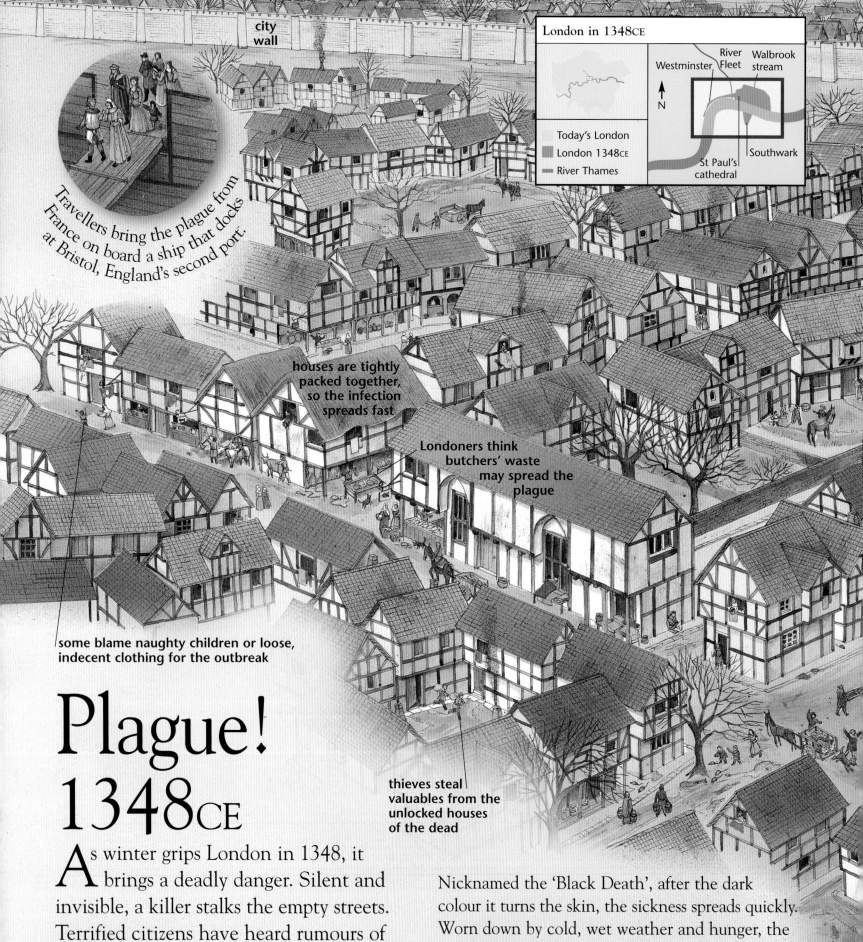

London in 1348CE

Westminster · River Fleet · Walbrook stream
N
Today's London
London 1348CE
River Thames
St Paul's cathedral
Southwark

Travellers bring the plague from France on board a ship that docks at Bristol, England's second port.

houses are tightly packed together, so the infection spreads fast

Londoners think butchers' waste may spread the plague

some blame naughty children or loose, indecent clothing for the outbreak

thieves steal valuables from the unlocked houses of the dead

Plague!
1348CE

As winter grips London in 1348, it brings a deadly danger. Silent and invisible, a killer stalks the empty streets. Terrified citizens have heard rumours of the threat, and stay indoors, but this does not save them. One-quarter of London's people die. Their killer is the plague, the most deadly disease ever to strike the city.

Nicknamed the 'Black Death', after the dark colour it turns the skin, the sickness spreads quickly. Worn down by cold, wet weather and hunger, the city folk have little strength left to fight the illness. When they catch it, apple-sized swellings appear in their groin or armpits, they cough up blood and die within days. Doctors' 'cures', such as draining the blood, only make the plague sufferers die faster.

so many have died that some streets are now empty

the poor are buried by the dozen in vast pits outside the city walls

The plague kills young and old, rich and poor without mercy. Some who can afford to flee survive – but their escape helps to spread the disease beyond London. The worst hit are those in crowded, stinking slums. At first, families bury their dead in local churchyards, but as the bodies pile up Londoners dig large pits to serve as mass graves. The plague ends in the spring, but there will be four more epidemics before the end of the century.

Three cold, wet summers in a row have ruined the harvests, so many Londoners are almost starving.

corpse carriers take dead bodies to mass burial sites

wealthy people flee, and spread the plague elsewhere

cold, wet weather means people are weak and hungry

In the plague pits of East Smithfield, as many as 200 victims share each huge grave.

the city has no sewage system – diseases breed in the filthy streets

only the wealthy get individual graves

space for graves will soon run out in the churchyards

religious people flog themselves to beg for God's mercy

even the poorest citizens are given a proper Christian burial

hungry dogs run amok

fleas on black rats may be spreading the plague

medical 'cures' do not work

21

The age of print 1476CE

At the back of a shop, in the shadow of Westminster Abbey, a worker heaves on a lever and inky metal letters squeeze against wet paper. Peeling off the page, he hangs it up to dry with lots of other printed sheets. Bound into books, the pages he is printing are transforming London – and Britain. They are spreading knowledge faster and further than ever before.

The owner of the workshop is William Caxton. A merchant and writer, he learned the secret of printing in Germany, where it was invented 40 years ago. Before then, books were rare and very expensive, because priests and monks had to write out every word by hand. Caxton's presses can print a thousand books in the time it takes to copy one with a pen.

all over Westminster it is green with meadows and farmland – and farm animals are still a common sight

the monks of nearby Westminster Abbey give money to support the Almonry residents

Westminster Abbey

the gardens are planted with herbs and divided up with criss-cross paths

printed books have made learning easier for boys at Westminster and other schools

a wooden press squeezes paper on to the inked type

Caxton's workshop is in the Almonry – a courtyard of shops, and houses for the poor

drying sheets of printed paper

the typesetter arranges tiny lead letters, called type, into words and sentences

the printer dabs ink on to the metal type using leather pads

herb clippings, known as 'strew', are thrown on to indoor floors to sweeten the stale air

22

William Caxton (c. 1415–92) is the first to print books in the English language.

London in 1476CE

Westminster
St Paul's cathedral
N
Today's London
London 1476CE
River Thames
Tower of London
Southwark

Westminster is royal London: King Edward IV (1442–83) has his palace close to Caxton's shop.

the Palace of Westminster, by the river, is the king's London home

the City of London lies about 2km to the east

St Paul's cathedral

scribes copying books by hand fear they will lose their jobs because of the new printing press

Westminster Hall

the King's Bridge

Royal Chancery

Organized in 'guilds', London's traders and craftworkers keep tight control over the city's businesses.

a gardener is clipping the hedges to gather 'strew'

by following every path, visitors can exercise in a small area

Thames lightermen (barge operators) bring paper from London's docks further downriver

The printing press makes book production cheaper, so more people than ever before are learning to read. It enables scientists to tell people about what they learn, leading to a revolution in discovery and invention. By taking bookmaking out of the church and monastery, printing will also help to spread new ideas about religion.

Caxton imports his paper from France and Italy

23

dumped rubbish and sewage block the smelly Fleet river

the River Thames is the city's main transport route

Baynard's Castle is a royal palace: the keeper entertained the queen with a banquet and firework display here

many of the theatres cluster on the south bank of the river, outside the control of the city council

William Shakespeare (1564–1616) writes 38 plays in all, and becomes the world's most famous playwright.

ferrymen bring theatre-goers across the river

the Rose was the first theatre to be built on Bankside, in 1586–7

the Globe and Rose theatres often compete with each other for audiences

Shakespeare belongs to a theatre company called the Lord Chamberlain's Men

Rose theatre

street vendor

to stand in the theatre costs one penny, to sit costs two, and for three pence spectators get a seat with a cushion

doughnut-shaped playhouse gives all a good view

Globe theatre

young male actors play all the female parts

the roof over the stage keeps the rain and sun off the costumes, some costing £15,000 in today's money

standing spectators are known as 'groundlings' or 'stinkards'

hazelnut shells stop the ground getting muddy when it rains

building materials for the theatres came from another dismantled theatre in north London

Shakespeare is also part-owner of the Globe theatre

Shakespeare's London 1602CE

As the actors appear on the stage, the chattering crowd falls silent. They have dragged themselves across the river to see a play, paying twice the normal price. It is the first public performance of *Twelfth Night* and they want to hear every word. Beside the stage, the playwright, William Shakespeare, smiles with satisfaction: another full house...

monks from an abbey in Surrey stay at Chertsey House when they visit London

Formed last year in a London pub, the East India Company will first trade with India, then rule it.

Broken Wharf got its name because it crumbled while its two owners argued for 40 years over the cost of repairs

St Mary Overie's Dock

Bankside's entertainment includes bear-baiting pits, where bears are chained up and made to scrap with hunting dogs

English people will look back on Elizabeth I's reign (1558–1603) as a 'golden age' of prosperity and culture.

people watch their step in these streets, because there are no lavatories in the theatres

His company have built a theatre, the Globe, at Bankside. This is a rough area of drunkenness and crime – but it is beyond the control of London's councillors, who say actors are no better than tramps who spread disease, noise and disorder. Their queen, Elizabeth I, disagrees. Though old, and tired by more than 40 years on the throne, she loves the theatre, and gives support to Shakespeare's company.

Others are also benefitting from the queen's interest. Her long reign has made London more wealthy. Ships from the Thames have defeated an invading Spanish fleet. City merchants have set up one of Europe's first stock exchanges. Their expeditions have explored the world, bringing its riches back to London. Sitting in the Globe theatre's best seats, these wealthy traders will applaud wildly at the play's end.

London in 1602CE

Westminster

St Paul's cathedral

N

Today's London
London 1602CE
River Thames

Baynard's Castle

Southwark

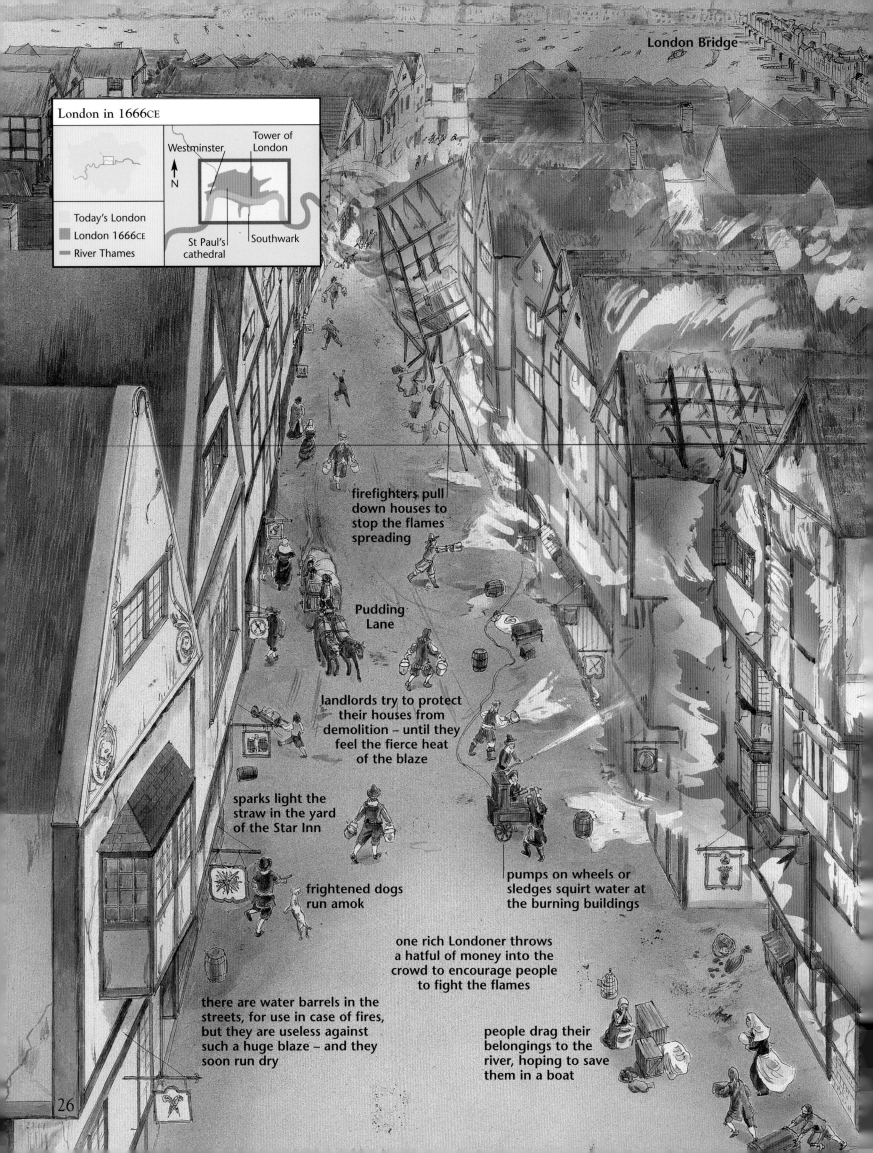

London in 1666CE

Westminster

Tower of London

N

St Paul's cathedral

Southwark

Today's London
London 1666CE
River Thames

London Bridge

firefighters pull down houses to stop the flames spreading

Pudding Lane

landlords try to protect their houses from demolition – until they feel the fierce heat of the blaze

sparks light the straw in the yard of the Star Inn

frightened dogs run amok

pumps on wheels or sledges squirt water at the burning buildings

one rich Londoner throws a hatful of money into the crowd to encourage people to fight the flames

there are water barrels in the streets, for use in case of fires, but they are useless against such a huge blaze – and they soon run dry

people drag their belongings to the river, hoping to save them in a boat

26

Southwark

the fire melts the bells in city churches

floating sparks ignite the dry thatch roofs

the streets are so narrow that flames can lick straight across them – and spread the fire

the baker and his family escape across the roofs

upper floors are built outwards, narrowing the streets further

scared of heights, the baker's maid stays behind – and burns

the wooden buildings burn quickly

the weatherproof coat of pitch, on the bakery walls, catches fire easily

sailors blow up houses to create firebreaks, which will stop the flames from spreading

the fire started at Thomas Farriner's bakery in Pudding Lane

The Great Fire 1666CE

Hot and crackling, yellow tongues of flame lick from the windows of a bakery on Pudding Lane. Just after midnight, on 2 September, a tiny spark from the oven has lit bundles of dry twigs stacked nearby. Within an hour, the blaze spreads to the whole of the street. Then the flames ignite nearby warehouses storing oil, spirits and pitch.

At first, few Londoners worry. Fires are common. Even the mayor is not concerned: he takes a good look at the fire and goes back to bed, thinking it is not a problem. He is wrong. A strong wind fans the flames. Buckets of water, the only common fire precaution, cannot quench them. When the fire reaches London Bridge it burns the water wheels that pump vital river water all over the city.

Writer Samuel Pepys (1633–1703) describes the fire in his diary: he buries his best cheese to save it.

Ferrymen helping families escape across the river make a healthy profit by doubling their fares.

As soon as it is clear their city is doomed, Londoners begin to flee. Taking only what they can carry, they escape across the river on a fleet of boats. Just six die. From the south bank, they watch for three days as a circle of flame eats up nine-tenths of their homes and possessions. But even before the ashes are cold, London's leaders are planning a new city.

From the ashes 1707 CE

The destruction of London, more than 40 years ago, was not all bad news. The flames swept away crowded, filthy, unhealthy streets. In their place, Londoners built a new, finer city. Inns and houses were first to be built, to new safety codes, using fireproof materials. They lined most of the burned streets just six years after the fire.

Public buildings were trickier. Officials turned down several designs for a grand grid of new avenues. Instead they sketched in the city hall, stock exchange, customs house and merchants' halls on roads that followed ancient routes. A tax on coal paid for the rebuilding work. To replace more than 50 churches lost in the flames they called on the gifted scientist and architect, Christopher Wren.

Christopher Wren (1632–1723) shared his work on the churches with several other architects.

This huge task has taken up half of Wren's life, but now it is almost complete. The last church to be finished is the biggest: St Paul's. To watch masons and carpenters working at dizzy heights, Wren is hoisted to the top in a basket. He is keen to check the details of the cathedral's crown – an immense dome. With a grey lead skin, it will become one of London's – and Britain's – most famous landmarks.

all roofing materials are now fireproof

wooden structures are forbidden – walls are now brick or stone

the old, ruined cathedral was demolished using controlled explosions, which locals mistook for earthquakes

the streets are now wider, but most still trace the pattern they followed before the fire

the centre-line of the cathedral lines up exactly with the rising sun on Easter morning

tired of people interfering, Wren hides the construction site behind huge wattle screens

wooden crane

the stones had to be winched up a hill from the river – the largest took one week to move

the total cost of construction is £736,000

workers are paid not by the hour, but by the foot of work completed

work on St Paul's cathedral, the largest burned building, began only when most other buildings were complete

the site is guarded by watchmen and two large mastiff dogs

just months before the Great Fire, Wren had suggested adding a dome to the old St Paul's

a cross is being erected at the top, 111m above the ground

Wren alters the details of the cathedral, and its dome, while the work is in progress

The finished cathedral is very different from the plans that Wren drew up to get his designs approved.

a wooden frame supports the outer dome

a supporting cone is made of brick

the smaller, inner dome is the cathedral ceiling

two huge iron chains ring the twin domes to stop their bases from spreading

lead outer skin

In the 1680s and 90s, the winters were often cold enough to hold fairs on the frozen Thames.

a whisper inside the gallery can be heard clearly on the other side, 33m away

London in 1707CE

Westminster Abbey

Tower of London

N

Today's London
London 1707CE
River Thames

St Paul's cathedral

Southwark

at the peak of construction, 400 men are at work on the site

workers digging foundations for new buildings unearth thick charcoal – a residue of wood burned in the Great Fire

29

Georgian London 1783CE

England's King George III (1738–1820) rules his realm from a divided city. It is not a high wall that cuts London in two, but money and class. Wealthy, noble Londoners live luxuriously in the grand new houses that are springing up everywhere. Yet in the mean streets nearby, children roam the streets in packs, like wolves, and have to steal to eat.

Businessmen meet in London's coffee houses (cafés) to exchange news and gossip, and do deals.

drovers herd geese from Wales to the London markets

smart houses, but no shops, line fashionable Oxford Street

a highwayman is being driven to the gallows at Tyburn – to be hanged

huge crowds follow the cart to watch the execution

Hangings at Tyburn are like festivals: people take the day off to watch criminals die.

rich Londoners take carriages to their gambling clubs

London's worst slums cluster around the church of St Giles. It is in this neighbourhood that the two sides of London come face to face. Of every ten children born here, just one will live to five years of age – and will probably survive by picking the pockets of the wealthy. If caught, that child will die on the gallows. At this time, brutal laws punish even minor crimes with execution.

wealthy people risk being robbed in broad daylight

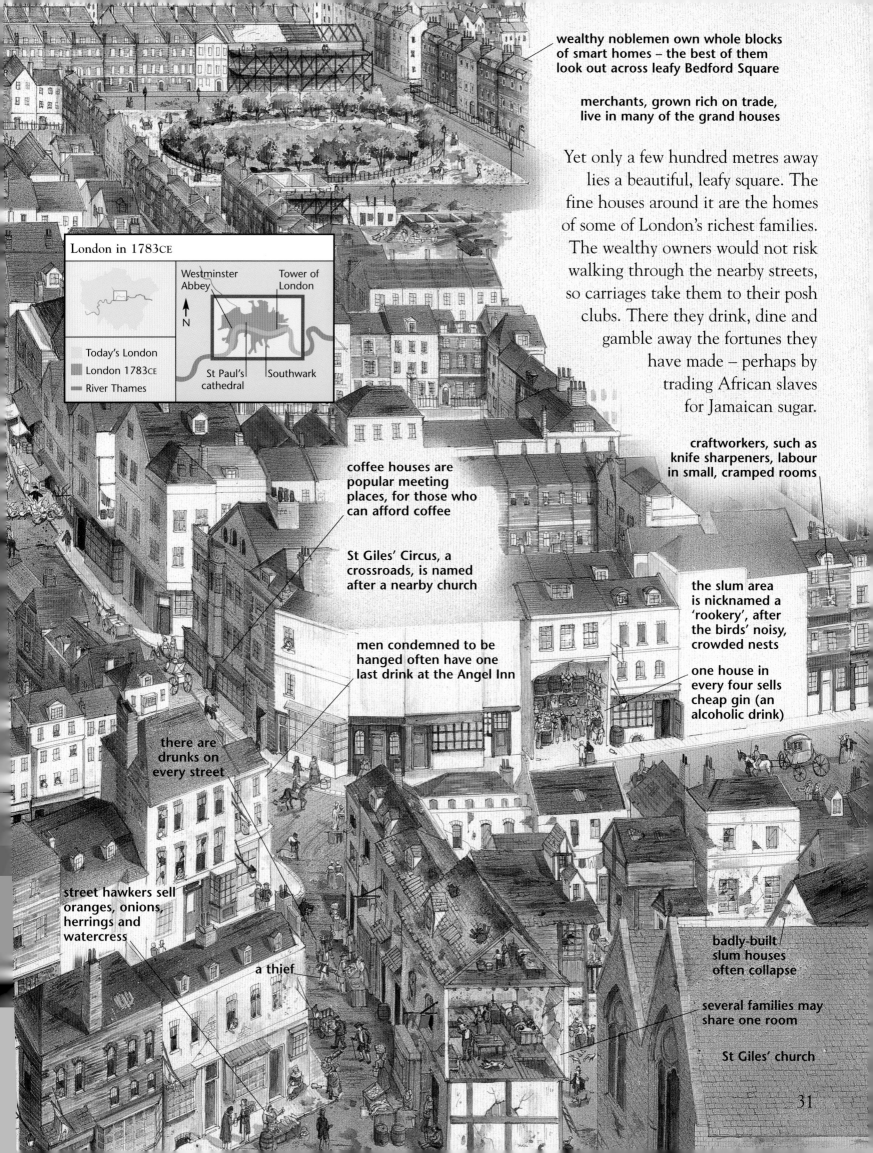

wealthy noblemen own whole blocks of smart homes – the best of them look out across leafy Bedford Square

merchants, grown rich on trade, live in many of the grand houses

Yet only a few hundred metres away lies a beautiful, leafy square. The fine houses around it are the homes of some of London's richest families. The wealthy owners would not risk walking through the nearby streets, so carriages take them to their posh clubs. There they drink, dine and gamble away the fortunes they have made – perhaps by trading African slaves for Jamaican sugar.

London in 1783CE

Westminster Abbey
Tower of London
N
St Paul's cathedral
Southwark

Today's London
London 1783CE
River Thames

coffee houses are popular meeting places, for those who can afford coffee

St Giles' Circus, a crossroads, is named after a nearby church

craftworkers, such as knife sharpeners, labour in small, cramped rooms

men condemned to be hanged often have one last drink at the Angel Inn

the slum area is nicknamed a 'rookery', after the birds' noisy, crowded nests

one house in every four sells cheap gin (an alcoholic drink)

there are drunks on every street

street hawkers sell oranges, onions, herrings and watercress

a thief

badly-built slum houses often collapse

several families may share one room

St Giles' church

31

The Great Exhibition 1851 CE

Glittering like a diamond in London's biggest park, the 'Crystal Palace' looks like a gigantic greenhouse. Though there are some plants – and even trees – inside, the crowds flocking through the doors swiftly pass these by. For this magnificent structure has been built to house an extraordinary exhibition, showing off the arts and industries of Britain and the rest of the world.

Architect Joseph Paxton (1803–65) modelled the Crystal Palace on a water-lily greenhouse.

the River Thames snakes off to the southeast

the design of the Crystal Palace is based on a garden greenhouse

the top panes of glass are as high as an eight-storey building

standard-sized parts were used in the construction, to speed up the building work

the giant glasshouse is big enough to enclose whole elm trees

at 564m, the building is longer than six soccer pitches

even with 93,000 people inside, the halls never seem crowded

laid flat, the glass panes would cover about 320 tennis courts

the visitors number six million in total – about one-third of Britain's population

entry to the exhibition costs one shilling – one-third of a labourer's daily wages

a London omnibus

Suggested by Prince Albert, husband of Queen Victoria (1819–1901), the Exhibition is a spectacular success. Every major nation has sent exhibits. Visitors gasp at the giant steam-powered machines, they wonder at marvels such as a piano for four players, and they laugh at sculptures made out of soap. One-third of Britain's people visit: their tickets not only pay for the show, but provide enough extra money to build three new museums nearby.

The Crystal Palace itself is as much a source of wonder as what is inside. It has been built in just nine months, using a cast-iron frame and glass sheets. When the show ends it will be taken down, moved 12km and reconstructed. A source of great pride for Londoners, the building and exhibition seem to sum up their city and country: wealthy, grand, proud and powerful.

London in 1851CE

Westminster Abbey
Tower of London
N
Today's London
London 1851CE
River Thames
St Paul's cathedral
Southwark

A display of moving machinery demonstrates how to save on human labour in industry.

profits from the exhibition will pay for new museums in nearby South Kensington

14,000 different exhibitors are putting their goods on display

The queen opens the show twice: once in Hyde Park, and again when it is moved to south London.

even the world's largest diamond, called the Kohinoor, is on show inside the Crystal Palace

the American exhibit, the biggest in the show, includes a huge piano – for up to four pianists – and sculptures made of soap

most of the machines on show are steam-powered – engineers refer to electric machines as 'toys'

visitors are excited by the gigantic size of the exhibition

boatbuilders and timber yards rely on the river for trade and deliveries

Strand Bridge, or Waterloo Bridge

electricity powers the modern flour mills

molten lead, poured from the high shot tower, forms tiny pellets for shotguns

carts pulled by huge horses deliver beer from the brewery

the Embankment (riverside) area was one of the first places in Britain to have electric street lights

a bridge carries the railway across the Thames to Charing Cross Station

trains from Waterloo Station connect the capital to south and southwest England

London is home to the world's first underground railway. More are being built to reduce road traffic.

a 'funeral train' takes coffins to a cemetery outside London

horses still pull even the biggest vehicles

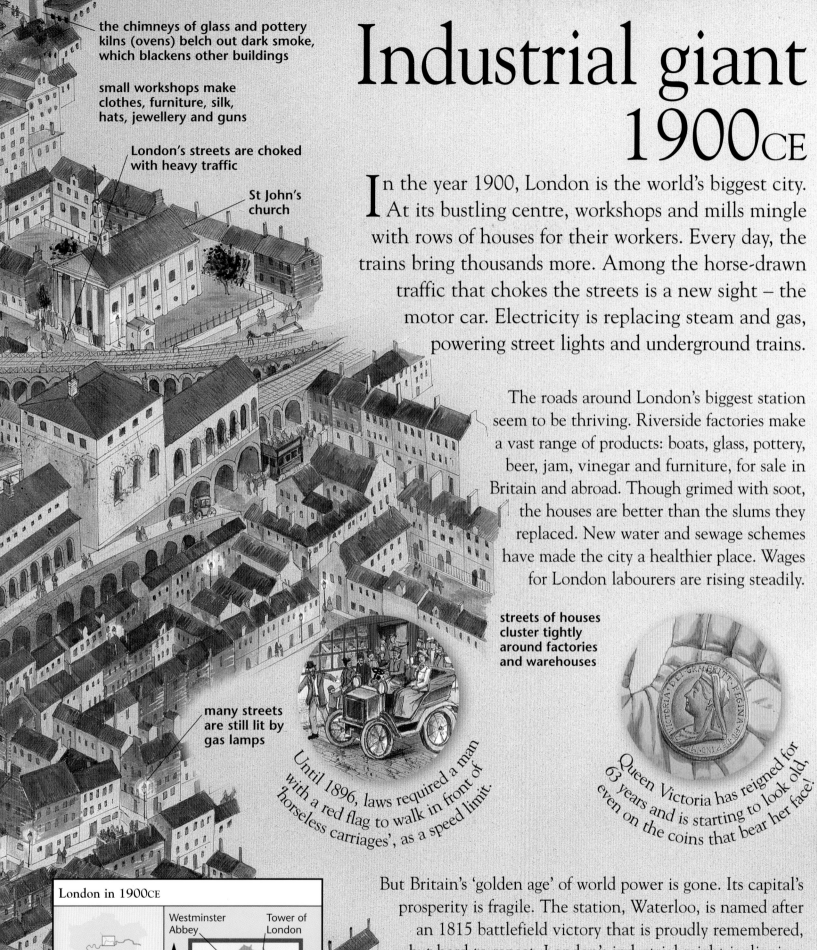

the chimneys of glass and pottery kilns (ovens) belch out dark smoke, which blackens other buildings

small workshops make clothes, furniture, silk, hats, jewellery and guns

London's streets are choked with heavy traffic

St John's church

Industrial giant
1900CE

In the year 1900, London is the world's biggest city. At its bustling centre, workshops and mills mingle with rows of houses for their workers. Every day, the trains bring thousands more. Among the horse-drawn traffic that chokes the streets is a new sight – the motor car. Electricity is replacing steam and gas, powering street lights and underground trains.

The roads around London's biggest station seem to be thriving. Riverside factories make a vast range of products: boats, glass, pottery, beer, jam, vinegar and furniture, for sale in Britain and abroad. Though grimed with soot, the houses are better than the slums they replaced. New water and sewage schemes have made the city a healthier place. Wages for London labourers are rising steadily.

streets of houses cluster tightly around factories and warehouses

many streets are still lit by gas lamps

Until 1896, laws required a man with a red flag to walk in front of 'horseless carriages', as a speed limit.

Queen Victoria has reigned for 63 years and is starting to look old, even on the coins that bear her face!

But Britain's 'golden age' of world power is gone. Its capital's prosperity is fragile. The station, Waterloo, is named after an 1815 battlefield victory that is proudly remembered, but hard to repeat. London's industrial might is slipping, too. Fewer and fewer countries want their goods made in these factories. Soon the city and the nation will be struggling with bigger, better competitors – and enemies – abroad.

London in 1900CE

Westminster Abbey

Tower of London

N

St Paul's cathedral

Southwark

Today's London
London 1900CE
River Thames

Anti-aircraft guns rarely hit the bombers – until computerized aiming arrives, later in the war.

Deep underground railway tunnels are the only places Londoners can sleep soundly during the bombings.

searchlight beams comfort Londoners, but do not protect them from attack

the bombs are not usually accurate enough to hit small targets, such as a bridge or railway line

Blackfriars Bridge

glowing 'tracer' shells show the gunners where they are aiming

Waterloo Bridge

air-raid sirens at the top of tall posts warn when bombers approach

anti-aircraft guns

Hungerford Bridge

citizens file into underground air-raid shelters when the sirens sound

Waterloo Station

Families huddle in their gardens inside crude shelters made of sheet steel and earth.

for each person that the bombings kill, 35 more are made homeless

anti-aircraft guns are set up all over London

St Paul's cathedral survives the bombings all around it

London's dockland areas, to the east, are the main targets for the bombers

Southwark Bridge

the streets are unlit, to confuse the bomber pilots, and city cars have dimmed headlights

all citizens must carry a gas mask with them at all times

sandbags protect doors from the bomb blasts

Londoners welcome American soldiers, whose help will enable Britain to defeat Germany.

German bombers are guided to target sites by radio beams, so they can attack what they cannot see.

Later in World War II (1939–45), Germany will bombard London with crude rocket missiles called V-2s.

The moon rises over rain-swept London rooftops, sirens wail and powerful searchlights criss-cross the sky. The city is under attack! Britain is at war, and enemy aircraft are approaching with deadly cargoes of bombs. Clutching gas masks, Londoners scurry into underground shelters and jump at the sound of the first explosions, far to the east.

Londoners refer to the bombing as 'the Blitz', taken from a German word, *Blitzkrieg*, which means 'lightning war'. They give it this name because the bombers are from Germany, Britain's enemy in the war. The Blitz began two months ago, and has continued every night since. Though the bombers aim for the docks, many bombs miss their target and instead fall on London homes. In the worst night of the Blitz, 1,400 people will die.

Londoners suffer because their city is almost defenceless. There are not enough public bomb shelters, searchlights are too weak and the anti-aircraft guns are too few. In the black sky, British fighter planes cannot find the bombers. But the government controls news reports to make it seem as if London is resisting and refusing to be beaten. Encouraged, the citizens get on with their lives – and, luckily for London, the Blitz fails.

London in 1940CE

Westminster Abbey

Tower of London

N

Today's London

London 1940CE

River Thames

St Paul's cathedral

Southwark

Fame and fashion 1963CE

For a short time, in the 1960s, London is the capital of cool. Screaming music fans crowd into sell-out pop concerts. Everyone, everywhere, wants to wear clothes by London designers. Young Londoners lead a protest movement against war, and against the old-fashioned attitudes of the past. Meanwhile, celebrity photographers capture the whole scene in gritty black-and-white images.

The streets themselves have not changed very much. New buildings fill gaps left by wartime bombs, but the West End looks much as it did 50 years ago. Today, a 'ban-the-bomb' protest march fills the wide avenues. London's fashion centre is nearby. Carnaby Street, in the seedy Soho neighbourhood, is now home to trendy tailors and shops selling daring, pop-art frocks.

in 1963, 'ban-the-bomb' protests pave the way to an international treaty ending nuclear weapons testing above ground

the protesters block London's traffic

London's famous red 'hop on, hop off' Routemaster buses will continue to ferry passengers until 2005

this protest emblem has become an international symbol for 'Peace'

the demonstrators have marched from an atomic bomb factory at Aldermaston in southern England

London in 1963CE

Westminster Abbey

Tower of London

N

St Paul's cathedral | Southwark

Today's London
London 1963CE
River Thames

trendy coffee bars line the streets of Soho

a tailor called John Stephen made Carnaby Street fashionable when he opened shops here

the slim, colourful look of London designer clothing will change fashions worldwide

men are wearing colourful clothing for the first time in centuries

From Liverpool, northern England, The Beatles are making British rock and pop music a success worldwide.

London is a centre for new music, too. In a few months' time, a band called The Beatles will play at Soho's massive Palladium theatre and establish itself as a global supergroup. Music pours from sweaty pubs, clubs and coffee bars, too: jazz from Ronnie Scott's, rock and roll from the Marquee and the 2i's coffee bar. Crowded with London's young, fashionable, well-dressed rebels, these cool venues make the city into one of the most 'happening' places on the planet.

its international fame will soon turn Carnaby Street into a popular tourist attraction

Groups of fashionable Londoners, known as 'mods', wear smart Italian suits and ride zippy Italian scooters.

Fashion designers are also setting up new boutiques along the exclusive King's Road in Chelsea, west London.

homes, photographers' studios, galleries and tailors' workshops fill the floors above the Soho boutiques

fashionable mods flock to Soho's clubs to dance to popular ska and soul music

passing underground, 'tube' trains gently shake the pavements

mods ride Italian motor scooters

small, affordable cars are making motoring much cheaper and more popular

London's streets were built for horses, so many are narrow for cars to use

at night, underground music swells from clubs in basements

39

Olympic city
Today

Neolithic people settled beside the Thames river because the high banks offered them safe homes and good hunting. Today, London's City – as its financial district is known – is attractive for similar reasons. The residents are very different, though. Bankers and business tycoons have made this a place where great wealth can be earned – and lost. In towering glass offices they hunt profits, not geese.

Once a Christian church, this City building became a Jewish synagogue, and now it is a Muslim mosque.

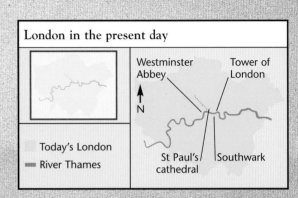

London in the present day

Westminster Abbey

Tower of London

N

St Paul's cathedral

Southwark

Today's London
River Thames

planners have preserved St Paul's cathedral and many other old City buildings

the 'square-mile' City is still London's main financial centre

rising property prices have driven factories out of London's centre

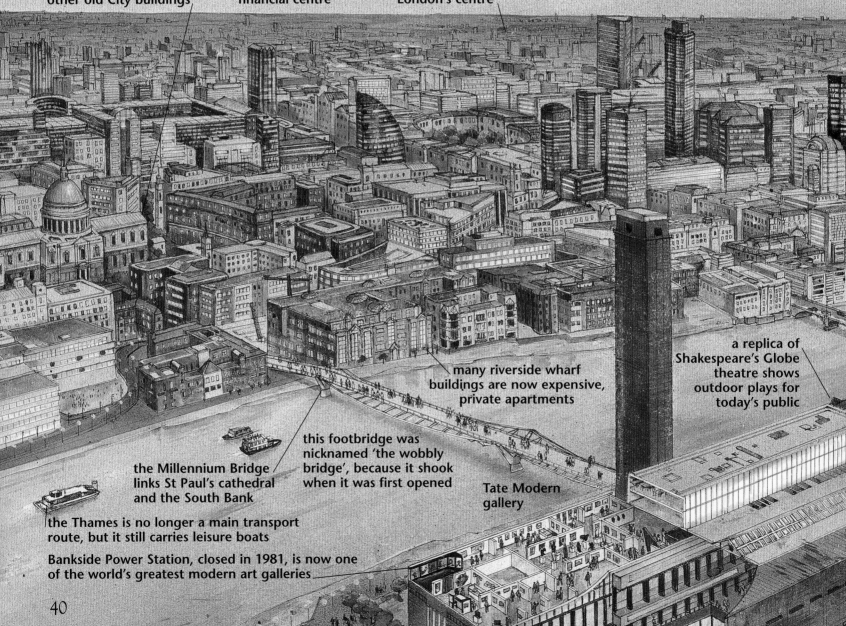

a replica of Shakespeare's Globe theatre shows outdoor plays for today's public

many riverside wharf buildings are now expensive, private apartments

this footbridge was nicknamed 'the wobbly bridge', because it shook when it was first opened

the Millennium Bridge links St Paul's cathedral and the South Bank

Tate Modern gallery

the Thames is no longer a main transport route, but it still carries leisure boats

Bankside Power Station, closed in 1981, is now one of the world's greatest modern art galleries

London now spreads out far beyond the City. Outside its ancient walls is a thriving, modern capital. Centuries of trade, migration and conquest have made it a place of many faces and races. Refugees took shelter here, and then settled. They brought new art, language, food and culture with them, making London an exciting, vibrant place to live and work.

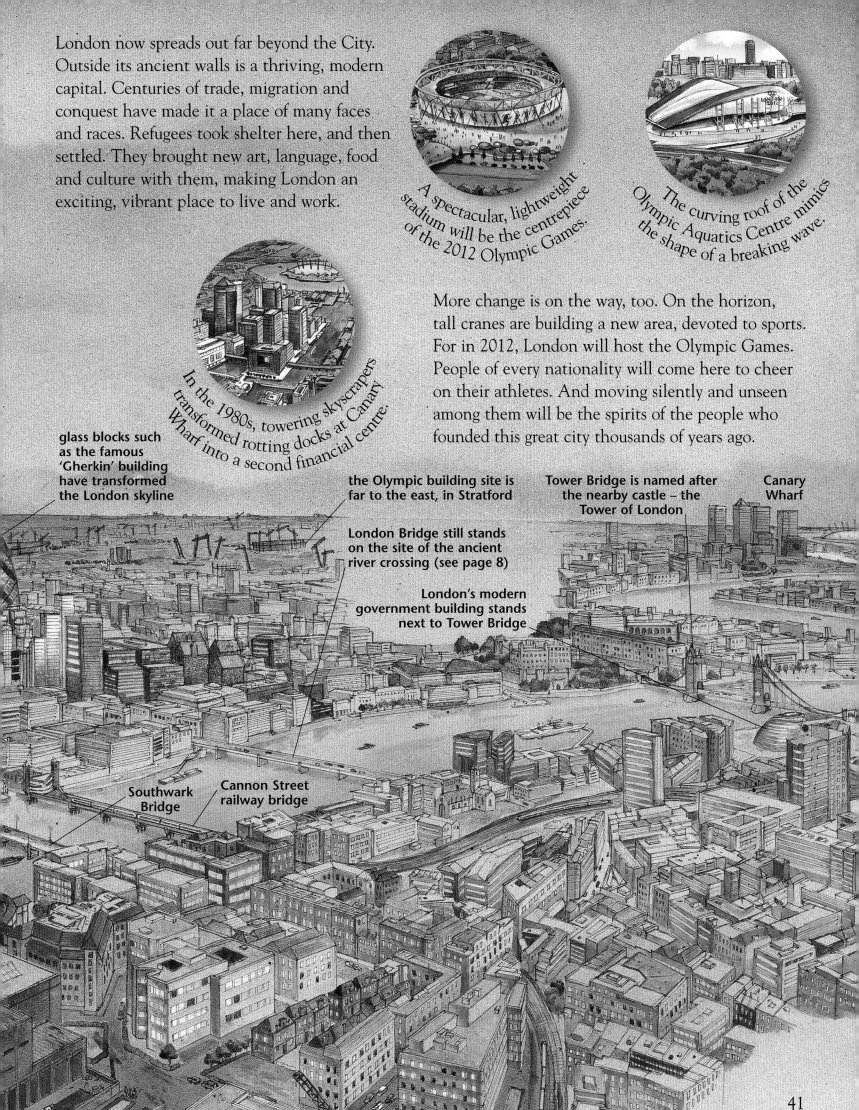

A spectacular, lightweight stadium will be the centrepiece of the 2012 Olympic Games.

The curving roof of the Olympic Aquatics Centre mimics the shape of a breaking wave.

In the 1980s, towering skyscrapers transformed rotting docks at Canary Wharf into a second financial centre.

More change is on the way, too. On the horizon, tall cranes are building a new area, devoted to sports. For in 2012, London will host the Olympic Games. People of every nationality will come here to cheer on their athletes. And moving silently and unseen among them will be the spirits of the people who founded this great city thousands of years ago.

glass blocks such as the famous 'Gherkin' building have transformed the London skyline

the Olympic building site is far to the east, in Stratford

Tower Bridge is named after the nearby castle – the Tower of London

Canary Wharf

London Bridge still stands on the site of the ancient river crossing (see page 8)

London's modern government building stands next to Tower Bridge

Southwark Bridge

Cannon Street railway bridge

41

Glossary

Words in *italics* refer to other glossary entries.

Aethelwulf (c. 795–858)
A *Saxon* king of southern England, who fought *Viking* raids on his lands.

Albert, Prince (1819–1861)
The husband of *Queen Victoria* who helped to plan London's Great Exhibition of 1851.

amphitheatre
A rounded stadium in which *Roman gladiators* fought to amuse spectators.

ancestor
Someone's parents, and also their grandparents and great-grandparents, and so on, through to the oldest members of a family.

Bankside
An area of the south bank of the *Thames* river, just west of *London Bridge*.

basilica
A building, usually found next to a *forum* in *Roman* cities, used for administration.

Black Death
A deadly *plague* that first struck Europe in the mid-14th century CE, killing up to half its population.

Blitz
A short form of *Blitzkrieg*, used to describe the German bombing of London in *World War II*.

Blitzkrieg
A German word meaning 'lightning war'.

Boudicca (or Boadicea, died c. 60CE)
The queen of the *Iceni* tribe, who attacked and burned the Roman city of *Londinium* in 60CE.

boutique
A small, fashionable shop that is not part of a chain of shops.

These simple Neolithic huts were built more than 5,500 years ago.

The Romans used African elephants to frighten and trample their enemies.

Britons
The people of Britain.

Caxton, William (c. 1415–92)
An English merchant and printer who was the first to print and publish books in English, in 1473.

Celts
A people from central Europe, who settled in Britain in the 9th century BCE.

Thames lightermen delivered paper to William Caxton's printing house.

chariot
A two-wheeled, horse-drawn war cart for carrying soldiers.

Christian
Someone who follows the religion begun by Jesus of Nazareth (born 7–2BCE; died 26–36CE), and worships him as the son of God.

City (of London)
The original, walled area that London occupied; and later, the financial and banking district.

civil war
A war between people of the same country.

conquest
The capture and rule of a country or city by its foes, using force.

crusades
The campaigns in the 11th to 13th centuries CE by *Christian* soldiers to free the holy land of Palestine from Muslim rule.

cursus
A *Neolithic* avenue of two straight ditches and banks, probably used as part of a religious *ritual*.

customs house
A building used for the collection of taxes on goods carried across a country's border.

daub
A mud coating for walls, smeared
on to *wattle*.

Neolithic pots

drover
Someone who drives farm animals,
usually to the marketplace in town.

East India Company
A British company, formed in 1600 to trade with
India, that eventually grew to control India.

Edward IV (1442–83)
The king of England from 1461. Edward's rule was
broken for six months by a rebellion in 1470–1.

Elizabeth I (1533–1603)
The queen of England and Ireland from 1558
until her death. Elizabeth's rule helped to make
her country wealthy and powerful.

epidemic
A serious outbreak of a disease in which many
people fall ill or die.

firebreak
An area deliberately cleared of anything that
might burn, in order to stop a fire spreading.

Fleet (river)
A small river that runs into the *Thames*, once used
for dumping rubbish, now hidden below ground.

forum
The marketplace and central
open space of a *Roman* town.

a Black Death burial pit

game
Wild birds and animals hunted
for food.

George III (1738–1820)
The king of Great Britain from 1760 until his
death. During George's reign, Britain's American
settlers rebelled to form the United States.

gladiator
A slave trained to fight in combats staged
in a *Roman amphitheatre*.

Globe theatre
A round wooden theatre
on *Bankside* where the *Lord
Chamberlain's Men* performed.

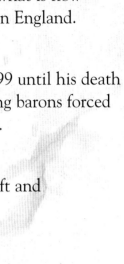
William Shakespeare's
Globe theatre

guild
A medieval organization in
charge of a particular trade.

Iceni
A tribe of *Celts* who lived in what is now
Norfolk and Suffolk, in eastern England.

John, King (1167–1216)
The king of England from 1199 until his death
in a *civil war*. Britain's rebelling barons forced
John to sign the *Magna Carta*.

lead
A heavy, grey metal that is soft and
easy to shape.

lighterman
A sailor who ferries goods on rivers using
a flat-bottomed barge.

Londinium
The *Roman* name for London.

London Bridge
The name for the first bridge to cross the
Thames river in London, and for all later
bridges on roughly the same spot.

Lord Chamberlain's Men
The theatre company of which *William
Shakespeare* was a member.

Louis VIII (1187–1226)
The king of France who briefly ruled half
of England in around 1216.

Lundenwic
The name for London when the city was controlled
by *Saxons* in the 7th and 8th centuries CE.

Magna Carta
A document limiting the power of *King John*, which
England's barons forced him to sign in 1215.

mason
A worker who cuts and lays the stones used to construct buildings.

Mediterranean
The region around the Mediterranean Sea, which separates southern Europe from North Africa.

migration
The movement of people between countries or continents.

a German *Heinkel He III* bomber from World War II

mithraeum
A temple for the worship of *Mithras*.

Mithras
A Persian god of light and truth, worshipped by *Romans* in the 1st century BCE.

mods
Originally a nickname for followers of modern jazz, in the 1960s 'mod' described people who dressed in designer clothes, and danced to popular music.

monastery
The home and place of work and worship for monks, men who live simple lives devoted to God.

mosque
A place of worship for Muslims, people who follow the religion of Islam.

New Stone Age
An ancient time period when people learned how to make finely-polished stone tools.

Neolithic
See *New Stone Age*.

nomadic
Wandering, with no fixed home.

Normandy
A region of northern France.

Normans
A French people from *Normandy* who conquered England in the 11th century CE, led by *William 'the Conqueror'*.

Palace of Westminster
The place where Britain's parliament meets, and the home of England's kings from the 11th to the 16th century CE.

Pepys, Samuel (1633–1703)
A naval officer who became famous for the diary he kept in London, over nine years, from 1660.

pitch
A thick, oily substance painted on walls and other surfaces to make them waterproof.

plague
A disease that spreads quickly and kills many people in a short time.

playwright
A person who writes plays.

pontoon
A temporary river bridge resting on boats or floats.

pop art
A style of art from the 1960s, using strong colours and bold images, often based on advertising, news or photographic images.

quay
A raised, waterside area where ships load and unload their goods.

refugee
Someone who goes abroad to find protection from religious or political turmoil in their home country.

ritual
Special actions repeated in a strict order, often as part of a religious service or ceremony.

Romans
A people from the city of Rome, who founded an empire that, by the 2nd century BCE, controlled England and much of Europe.

King Louis VIII travelled to London from France in 1216, and replaced the English king.

the White Tower
under construction

St Paul's cathedral
The largest and most important *Christian* church in the *City of London*.

Saxons
A German people who invaded Britain in the 5th century CE and settled there.

Shakespeare, William (1564–1616)
An actor and theatre manager in the *Lord Chamberlain's Men*, who became Britain's (and the world's) most famous *playwright*.

shells
Explosives fired from large guns.

a British anti-aircraft gun from World War II

Soho
A lively neighbourhood of small streets at the centre of London's West End, and a centre for eating, drinking and entertainment since the 19th century CE.

Southwark
A district of London, south of *London Bridge*.

stock exchange
A place where traders gamble on the future value of businesses, and by doing so raise money for the expansion of the same businesses.

synagogue
A temple of worship for Jews, people who follow the religion of Judaism.

Thames (river)
The large river that runs through London.

Tower of London
The castle built in the 11th century CE by the *Normans* at London's eastern corner.

Tyburn
A place in west London traditionally used for public executions (punishment killings).

V-2
A missile fired at London from the European mainland by the Germans during *World War II*.

Victoria, Queen (1819–1901)
England's queen from 1837 until her death, Victoria reigned for longer than any English ruler before or since.

Vikings
Seafaring people who raided European ships and coastlines from their Scandinavian bases, from the 8th to the 11th century CE.

Walbrook stream
A small river, now covered over, that once ran through the middle of the walled *City of London*.

wattle
A woven panel of twigs used in building, often coated with *daub*.

Westminster Abbey
The main church of Westminster, once the place of worship for a *monastery* located there.

wharf
See *quay*.

White Tower
The original *Tower of London*, later the largest of several buildings together enclosed by walls and the *Thames* river.

William 'the Conqueror' (c. 1028–87)
Originally named William of *Normandy*, a *Norman* duke who conquered England in 1066 and became the country's king.

World War II (1939–45)
A catastrophic six-year war in which Britain, the United States and their military allies fought an alliance that included Germany, Italy and Japan.

Wren, Christopher (1632–1723)
An English architect who designed a new *St Paul's cathedral*, and many other churches, after they were destroyed in the Great Fire of London, in 1666.

In 1900, most of the London traffic was still drawn by horses – including the large omnibuses.

Index

The last person to be executed at Tyburn, west London, was a highwayman called John Austin, in 1783.

Searchlights scanned the London sky for bombers during the Blitz of World War II.

For Heidi and Simon

First published 2009 by Kingfisher
an imprint of Macmillan Children's Books
a division of Macmillan Publishers Limited
The Macmillan Building, 4 Crinan Street, London N1 9XW
Basingstoke and Oxford
Associated companies throughout the world
www.panmacmillan.com

Consultant: Dr Hugh Clout, Department of Geography, University College London

Additional consultancy: John Clark at the Museum of London; Dr Richard Dennis,
Department of Geography, University College London; Maya Gabrielle and Gwilym Jones;
Paul Needham at the Scheide Library, Princeton University Library, Princeton, New Jersey, USA.

Additional illustration work by Monica Favilli and Cecilia Scutti

ISBN 978-0-7534-1733-1

1 3 5 7 9 8 6 4 2
1TR/0209/SHE/CLSN(CLSN)/158MA/C

A CIP catalogue record for this book is available from the British Library.

Printed in Taiwan

Westminster was the home of English
rulers from the 11th century until the
early 16th century.